INSIGHTS
from the
Heart

Tania Thornton

Copyright © 2013 Tania Thornton

Illustrated by Maureen McWilliams

All rights reserved. No part of this book may be used or reproduced by any means, graphic, electronic, or mechanical, including photocopying, recording, taping or by any information storage retrieval system without the written permission of the publisher except in the case of brief quotations embodied in critical articles and reviews.

ISBN: 978-1-4525-6685-6 (sc)
978-1-4525-6686-3 (e)

Library of Congress Control Number: 2013900801

Balboa Press books may be ordered through booksellers or by contacting:

Balboa Press
A Division of Hay House
1663 Liberty Drive
Bloomington, IN 47403
www.balboapress.com
1-(877) 407-4847

Because of the dynamic nature of the Internet, any web addresses or links contained in this book may have changed since publication and may no longer be valid. The views expressed in this work are solely those of the author and do not necessarily reflect the views of the publisher, and the publisher hereby disclaims any responsibility for them.

Any people depicted in stock imagery provided by Thinkstock are models, and such images are being used for illustrative purposes only. Certain stock imagery © Thinkstock.

Printed in the United States of America

Balboa Press rev. date: 02/22/2013

Acknowledgments

I would like to acknowledge and thank Louise Hay, and her book *How to Heal Your Life*, for it was through practicing my affirmations and incorporating those techniques into my daily living that my life was transformed. Bless you.

I would like to say a big thank you to my husband, Wayne. Without him empowering and loving me every day, this book would not have happened.

I would also like to say a special thank you to my dear friend Maureen for all the beautiful illustrations in this book.

To everyone else who has touched my life, I thank you for everything that you have done for me and bless you all.

Thank you for my life; if it had not happened like this, then I would not be the person I am today, sharing my insights and inspirations with others.

Foreword

When Tania asked me to peruse the draft of her first book, I was flattered. Not because of any literary talent or editing skills but having known her for a number of years I knew whatever she wrote would be a reflection of her high standards. She would have thought carefully before approaching anyone for this task. Like some Nordic warrior woman upholding the shield of truth against the rampages of war she forges forward with the confidence acquired from the many knock backs life has presented. She writes in an honest manner, open and vulnerable, presenting her insights to the world out of love and gratitude.

Her arrows fly straight to the heart of any matter offering warmth, comfort and encouragement when faced with difficult life experiences. The draft came at a moment when I needed to be reminded of the goodness in life. Just like a net having been cast onto the waves, the debris is teased apart leaving only that which is worthy. So it was when I read Tania's words and reacquainted myself with my Self. That is, this tired and dusty heart is fresh and green with new life restored by her gentle and straightforward reflection.

Maureen McWilliams

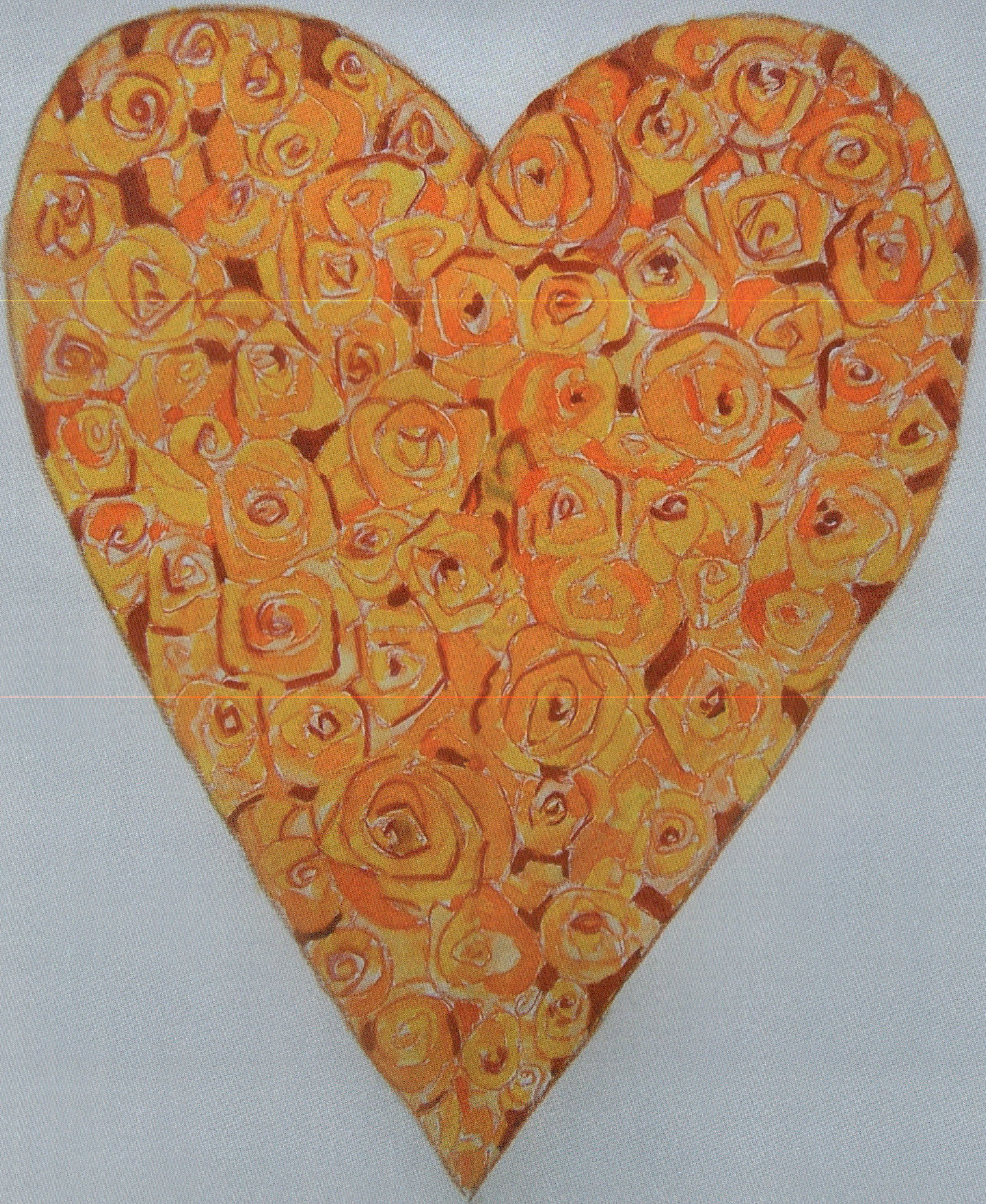

Preface

This book is an extension of my inner self, reaching out and hoping to touch, heal, and empower everyone who reads it.

Everyone on this planet is a unique individual. There is no other person in the universe like you. You are the one who lives your life every day regardless of what goes on around you. You and you alone know what is best for you, and your highest good.

There is a light inside of everyone, and when you let it out to shine, things do change for you. Listen to the song or watch the video "Firework" by Katy Perry. This song is spot-on.

Whatever your gifts are and wherever you need to shine them, let them shine. The power is within you. If you are in a place at this time where your gifts are unable to shine, then I would suggest that you invest in Louise Hay's book *How to Heal your Life*, as this will enable you to move to a different space.

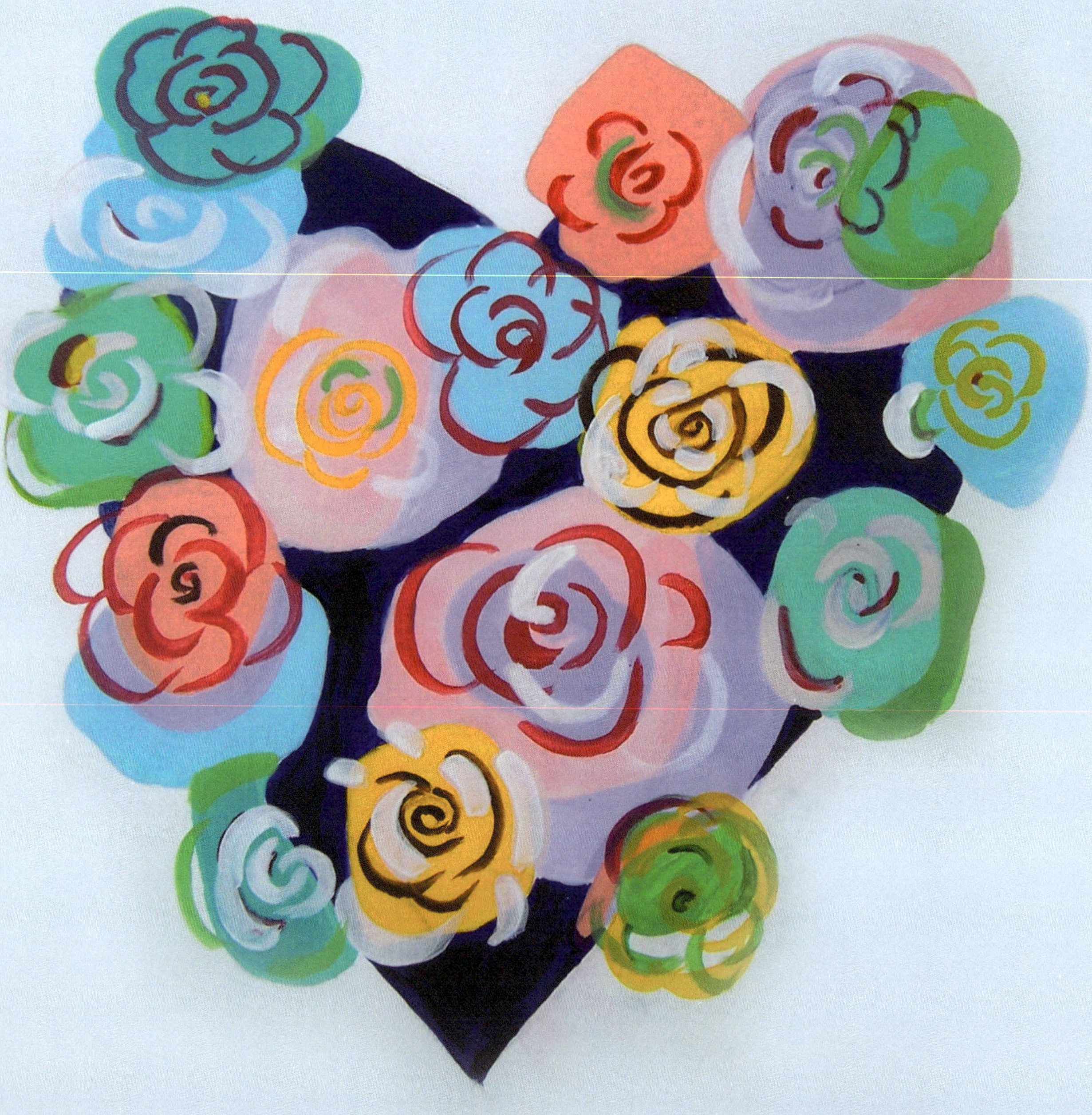

An Open Heart

A new day is dawning. I open my eyes.

I look out the window and see the sun rise.

Feeling scared and uncertain that life passes me by,

I take a deep breath and let out a sigh.

As the tears wash away all my hurts and my fears

And start to heal all my wounds from over the years,

I am on a new path now, one I can create.

My hopes and my dreams, I hand them to fate.

I open up my heart and feel the loving it brings.
Beating with love and understanding,
it gives me wings.

I open up my heart and feel the loving it brings.
Filled with kindness and compassion for so
many things.

Spreading my wings and growing each day,

Asking for my dreams to come true as I pray.

Living each moment as it unfolds,

With lots of love it all turns to gold

I open up my heart and feel the loving it brings.
Beating with love and understanding,
it gives me wings.

Being true to myself, no more second-best.

My heart leading me, I can ask for no more and no less.

Growing stronger inside me releases my pain.

Remembering that no one else is to blame.

I open up my heart and listen to what is within.
It starts with acceptance;
That's where I'll begin.

So listen to your heart

Inside. Believe in yourself.

So listen to your heart

Inside. Believe in yourself.

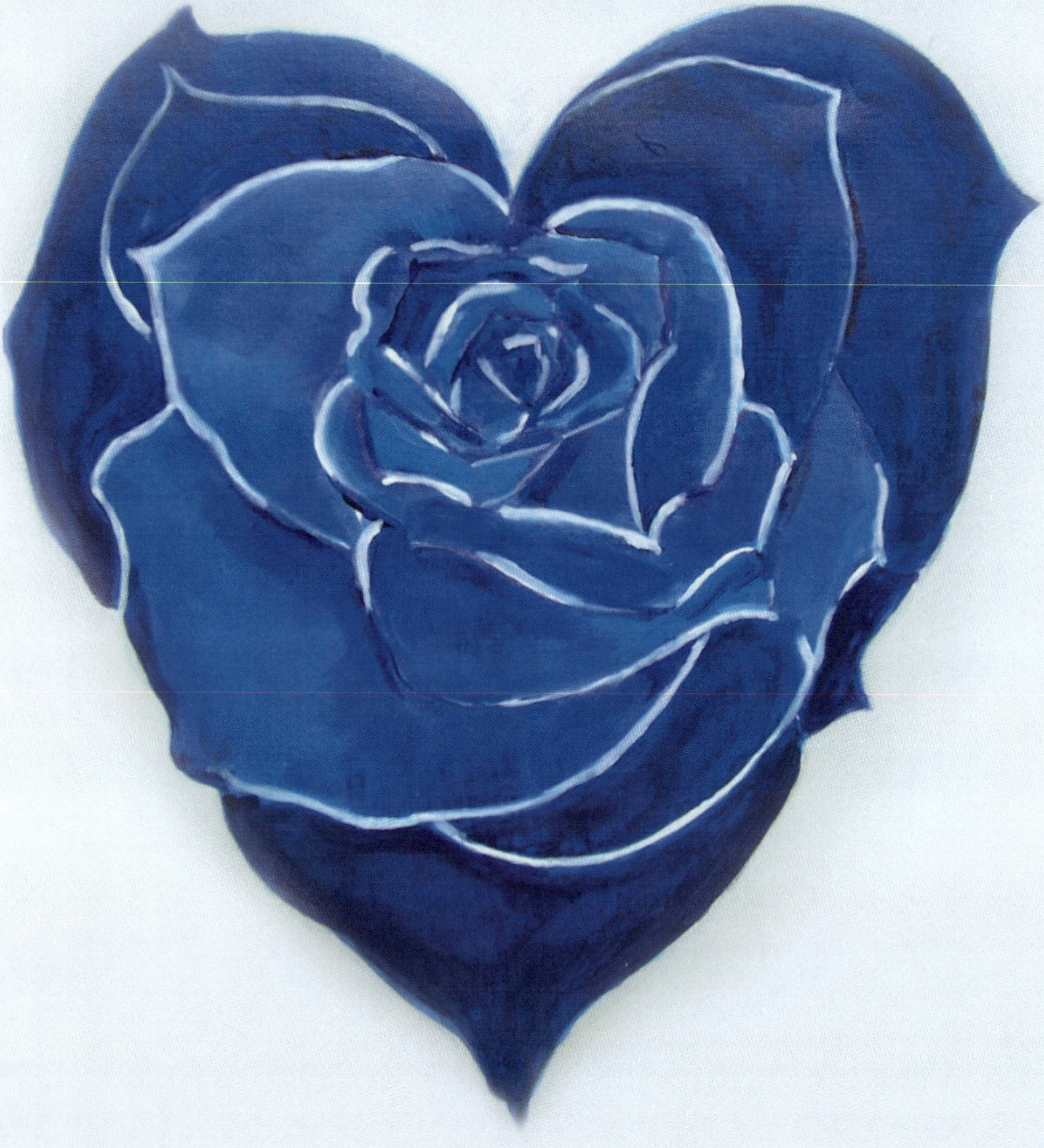

Contents

An Open Heart

1	My Life Story So Far	3
2	Love	13
3	A Mother's Love	19
4	Losing a Child	23
5	Losing Someone Close to You	25
6	A Father's Love	27
7	A Child's Unconditional Love	29
8	Your Inner Guidance System—Intuition	31
9	Being Present in Each Moment	33
10	Stress	35
11	Your Mind and Body's Ability to Heal Itself	37
12	My Healing Gifts	39
13	Your Spiritual Journey	43
14	Dreams Can Come True	45
15	Money	49
16	Relationships	51
17	Friends	55
18	Wounds	57

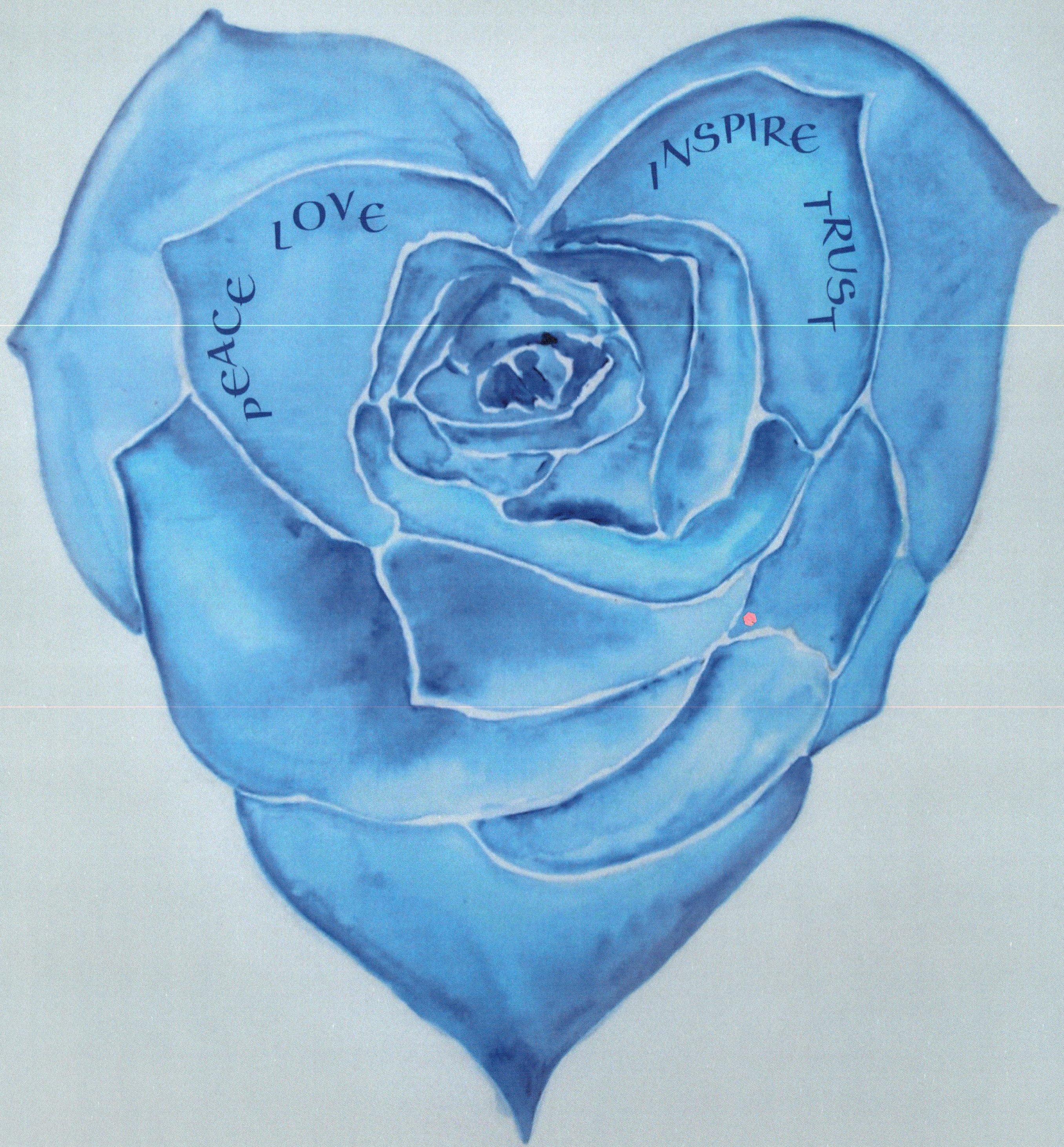
PEACE
LOVE
INSPIRE
TRUST

Chapter 1: My Life Story So Far

I was born in Auckland, New Zealand, and grew up in a suburb called Papatoetoe. I was the second eldest child; I have an older sister and two younger brothers. I was a bit of a tomboy. I had a bubbly personality and was quite cheeky, mischievous, fun, and outgoing. Growing up was quite a tough and confusing time for me. Our family did not have much money, and my dad worked two jobs to support us. Sometimes the stress of working those jobs and having a young family was too much, and he could be quite tough.

My mother was a good mother, providing lots of love although both my mum and dad were very strict. Even so, I am very grateful to my mother for being there for me when I was younger and making me feel loved. The fond memories I have were of all the animals we had in our house and the unconditional love. I remember that I would always bring home stray animals and there was one time when we had a dog, 3 cats, an aviary of birds, a goat, mice, guinea pigs, rabbits and goldfish. Living in an older cottage there was also a time when we had birds nesting in the roof and a hive of bumble bees in the wall. Yes we really did have the birds and the bees going on. My gran would visit us every weekend and she even taught me how to drive. She was a great gran, I still miss her but I know that she is here with me.

It was tough for a young girl growing up back then, as in those days little girls were seen and not heard. This was quite hard for a strong-willed, determined young miss who was probably a bit ahead of her time and often found herself in trouble, especially when things didn't go my way. I also had things going on with me that I didn't understand and was not allowed to talk about back then. I used to go to the Catholic Church Sunday School, which was not something that I enjoyed, where I was taught that any of the gifts that I had were a sin and anything I was seeing or hearing could not be brought out in the open. It was like I had a deep dark secret.

We were brought up that the man provided and the woman stayed home with the children. As I got older I knew that this was not what I wanted my role in the universe to be. I was quite strong and independent and liked earning money (and spending it as well) so I could do what I wanted to do. I did okay at school, but I did even better at secretarial school, and my career as a legal secretary began.

Because of my low sense of self-worth as a young woman, I would attract the wrong kind of men for me. I did not believe that I deserved anyone who would treat me with love and respect. The ones I did pick did not treat me well, being unfaithful and treating me as though I didn't exist and back then I did a lot of partying and drinking to block out the pain and although I had a lot of fun I was not truly happy with myself. I did not take care of myself, and my weight ballooned, but with all that going on I still managed to hold down a good job as a legal secretary and worked hard. During this time I always felt that I was worth more and somehow I managed to win $10,000.00 on a radio station. A police dog picked my envelope out of thousands of entries. I had a big party as I had heaps of friends, I bought a new car, lent my sister money to buy her house and went on a holiday. I had lots of friends around me who needed my help and I was always running around helping them, looking after their children as well as picking up their pieces. I was also Club Captain of a tennis club.

At this time I was a helpful, responsible young woman-on the outside I looked happy-but underneath I was not happy with how my life was. I learned a lot from this part of my life, I knew that I had clairvoyance and intuitive gifts but I was still too scared to use them.

One day I decided to make a change and when I turned twenty-eight I moved to Sydney. Being in a new country by myself, it was at this time, that I realised what my mum and dad had done for me and I knew that at the time both my parents did their very best for me and I was so grateful for the roof over my head, food on the table, an education, and for everything they were able to do for me in my lifetime, including spoiling me sometimes and the biggest thing for me was always knowing that I had a home to go home to. I love both of my parents very much and now understand the sacrifices that they made for me.

While in Sydney I got a good job with a law firm and I met my first husband. He was unable to read or write so he had a totally different outlook on the world. Although at first we thought we loved each other, it turned out that this relationship could not be sustained in a healthy mature way. After seven years of living in a marriage where I worked very hard to make it work, even after trying counseling, I realized that this marriage had become too hard and not very healthy for either of us. I was always pissed off, angry, and unhappy. I was a very loyal and naive wife, plus I was still in my program of the only way I felt I could love someone was trying to fix everything for them to make their lives better. At the time I did not realize that I needed to do this for myself as I am only responsible for myself and my actions.

One day I managed to have the strength to pack my bags and walk out. I never went back. I still had my job, but I had been left with my husband's debt as he had no money and my name was on the loan documents. It was only through the kindness of strangers and my boss at that time that helped me get back on my feet. This was my wake up call in life. This was my moment when life was to change for me forever.

I felt like the stuffing had been knocked out of me, I thought I was going to be married to the same person for the rest of my life. As I had been left with all this debt from my husband I thought there was something wrong with me, it was my fault, no one loved me and I had done something really wrong and I deserved to be punished. I was embarrassed and humiliated, feeling I had let everyone down and that I had failed. I remember my dad ringing me at this time and saying "Tania we are so proud of you because you did your very best to try to make the marriage work". Thanks dad but I still had not forgiven myself.

I needed somewhere to live and this particular day an ad was in the paper so I answered it and met Merv and Coora, they must have liked me because I moved in a week later. They were like my family. I lived in a very basic garage at the back of their house in Penrith for two years so I could pay off all the debt that was owing. After that time I finally had enough money to buy a car, and had finished paying off all the debt. It was like a weight had been lifted off my shoulders and I could move forward. I did not know about inner strength or where it comes from until this happened in my life. From a place of suffering came a lot of learning and I had to start to trust and have faith that everything was going to be okay no matter what happened. My spiritual journey had started.

After my divorce came through I decided, then and there, not to get involved with anyone else. I knew if I wanted my life to change, I was going to have to work with myself first. I had learned a lot about myself in my marriage and the patterns that were a part of me. If I wanted these patterns to stop repeating themselves then I was going to have to go within. I was in another country, with no family around, and the only support I had was the kindness of strangers that I had befriended or worked for and who helped me.

Today I am very thankful for the learnings I gained from this experience about people and life, which made me a more complete and compassionate person towards myself and others. At the time I didn't realise that we can create the things we think and talk about.

After that I joined the Spiritualist Church, met some lovely people who also helped me out, read books, and started to follow the teachings of *How to Heal Your Life* by Louise Hay.

I started to do my affirmations every day: "I am a good person," "I am worthy of the very best in the world," "I am grateful for everything that I have," "I trust that everything is happening for my highest good," "I am safe." This was a time of having faith and trusting that everything was going to be okay.

It was then my sister Maria said, "Why don't you move to Brisbane?" I thought about it and decided that yes this would be a good idea. So I did. I packed up all my stuff and sent it on a truck and I drove to Brisbane. Within two weeks I had a good job in a legal firm. And my life in Brisbane started. I was fortunate enough to be able to stay at my sister's for about six months, until I bought my first little unit in Brisbane. My dad and my sister helped me to purchase my unit, this meant I could move into my own place straight away and gave me the time I needed to pay them back. Our family have always been able to help each other out when it is needed. It was the first time that I felt very proud of what I had achieved.

My life had picked up and had started going really well. I had a good job working in a legal firm, joined the Spiritualist Church, and had started to do healings on people; I was accepting my clairvoyance as part of me, and it felt right. I had met a lovely friend, Angela, in Brisbane. I also had another friend, Maureen, the illustrator of this book, also psychic, who did readings for me. I had my very supportive cousin Leanne. And I had my cat Claude. I was reading my Louise Hay book and incorporating my affirmations into my life on a daily basis.

I found Brisbane a great city with the best weather. This was a good settling and grounding period for me, and I met a lot of nice, genuine like-minded people.

While I was in Brisbane, I was also doing some independent typing and an assignment came in from Inna Segal, asking me to type up all the interviews she had done with famous people. This work was inspiring and I got to hear first hand the interviews of Suze Orman, Uri Geller, Jack Canfield, and many other inspiring people. I now look back and see that this was all part of my journey. Although things were going really well in Brisbane I always felt that there was something deeper in my life that was missing.

In 2005 I went back to New Zealand for my brother's wedding and, while holidaying in Wellington, New Zealand, I met my husband, Wayne. We met in a mutual friend's coffee shop in Wellington for twenty minutes, and we did not know what would happen. It turns out that something did happen.

We would email each other every day, and then phone each other every night. Once a month one of us would cross the Tasman, and soon we knew that someone would have to move. (Yes, it turned out to be me.) It was a very special time in my life. I had no idea that this would happen to me, and when it did you could have pinched me, as it was like a fairy tale. Going to work and my relationship were the only things going on in my life at that point.

So once again I took a leap of faith and I rented my unit in Brisbane out and traveled across the Tasman and moved back to New Zealand, but to Wellington this time. The weather here is a bit of a challenge. (I was so proud of myself putting up my greenhouse one day, only to have the wind rip the cover and blow it down the next.) Wellington has other things to offer besides the weather. When it is a sunny day, you can't beat it, it is a beautiful day. After about 6 months I knew I was going to stay in Wellington so I sold my unit in Brisbane.

I got a good job and things were going well. Wayne was into drag racing and we had one fun filled year touring round New Zealand having a great time running the team for a Class 1 Dragracing Corvette.

We had been going out about a year and Wayne said that he wanted to get married and buy me a ring but he wanted me to pick the ring before he asked me. So we went out and picked the ring and all I asked was that when he decided to ask me that he would surprise me.

It was about a year after this and he still had not asked me to marry him and so one day I said, "How come you haven't asked me to marry you yet?" And he said "Every time I go to, you are a cow so I don't". I thought about this and left it alone.

One afternoon after going grocery shopping Wayne suggested that we go for a drive up to Mt Victoria to see the sights. I didn't think anything of it other than it was a bit spontaneous for Wayne. We got to the top and it was a beautiful day, you could see the planes flying in and out of the airport, there were people everywhere and I turned to him and said "This would be a great place for you to ask me to marry you as it is the first place you brought me to when I came to Wellington". He said "Funny you should say that" and he pulled out my engagement ring and said "Will you Marry Me", I was shocked and surprised but I managed to say "Yes". With that someone tapped Wayne on the shoulder and asked if he would take their photo so being the general good guy that he is, off he went and left me standing there.

We then had to tell everyone and when we visited our friends the Fallons in Auckland we were sitting around talking about where we could get married and Kerry suggested the Venetian Hotel in Las Vegas. We both thought that the idea sounded great. It could all be organized through the internet. We were off on another adventure! Las Vegas—who would have thought? We did have some drama as Wayne had been in a car accident the week before which left him battered and bruised and with torn rib cartilage. When we arrived in Las Vegas we found out that his bags had been left in Auckland. When we got to the hotel I became quite ill with vomiting and diarrhea. And so it went on. Security had to be called. It was just like on television. I was so sick and they arrived at the motel room in their uniforms with their guns and they said "Would you like the paramedics mam" with their strong American accents. I was so embarrassed I just wanted to hide away. Eventually we worked out that the best option was to get the hotel doctor to come and see me. He gave me an injection which managed to get me through the wedding day. Wayne's bags finally turned up half an hour before we had to leave to go to the wedding so at least he had something to wear.

Despite all the drama the wedding day was spectacular. We were treated like a king and queen. It was a very special day, and Wayne had our special friend Camp Stanley (American drag racer) attend the wedding and I managed to hold everything together. The day after the wedding the injection seemed to wear off and I became sick again. We rung the doctor who suggested that I needed to go to hospital. So we set off on our trip to The Desert Sands hospital in Las Vegas. This was an interesting experience and I still have my hospital socks and Wayne says that they are the most expensive socks in the world. After being tested for everything I was put on a drip and given a morphine injection which settled my whole system down and I was eventually able to be released. We had to change all our flights as we were flying out to LA that day. Once I had stabilised, we did fly to LA and we honeymooned in Disneyland (I loved Fantasyland) and San Diego (I loved San Diego SeaWorld). Even though I had become sick it really was a dream come true, I was lucky that I was still able to make the best of it while I was there regardless of how sick I was. (To me there is no other place in the world like Disneyland).

Wayne and I have been together for coming up seven years now, and he is my rock. I am his organizer and he says that I am quite strong and deep. I believe that a relationship takes work from both sides to strengthen it and that work needs to be done every day. We are both very honest with each other, and this gets us through the tough times (sometimes we both need to soften our honesty, but we work through it). I finally have a husband who loves and respects me, and the same is returned. Wayne and I have learned always to work together to create our future. Communication is the key to keeping your relationship happy and healthy and evolving to develop a deeper understanding of each other.

He is very supportive of my spiritual/clairvoyant side, and since he has been with me he has also made some significant changes within himself; we have been blessed to have grown together and our relationship has matured and become deeper. He is a very private person, while I have a very outgoing, bubbly personality.

I have a great job that I love with a truly fantastic boss. I bought him a paperweight with a Porsche on it because he truly is the Porsche of all bosses and I am blessed to have very supportive and loving people working around me. I am now running a successful healing business doing clairvoyant readings for people connecting with spirit to bring their loved ones through or help them with any life issues they may have. I am an open channel for my guides to work through. I am a qualified Reiki practitioner and also a Life Coach using my own life experiences to teach techniques to help clients release and clear past limiting beliefs and programs so they can move forward and deal with the stress of everyday life in a more positive and healthy way. I am trusting that the insights I share throughout this book will somehow touch the hearts of every reader who reads it to help their lives open up in a new way.

In this lifetime I have not been blessed to have children. We have even tried IVF, which did not work for us. The IVF process is rather invasive, and when it doesn't work it is heartbreaking for the people involved. We decided not to try it again. All I can suggest is before you go into it make sure you are aware of everything and if you are going through it I wish you the very best for a successful outcome. I am lucky because I have loved many children in my life and hope to love more in my lifetime.

I have a funny story about the IVF process though. Without all the technical terminology the IVF process is injections, scans, egg collection, insemination and then putting fertilized eggs back in the uterus. This particular day we were going to have egg collection done. We had to park quite a distance from the hospital as there was nowhere to park. A few unkind words were spoken and then we walked to the hospital. After having two eggs removed, I got dressed and went back to reception to meet Wayne. Being in some pain and discomfort Wayne said to me "Wait here and I'll go and get the car". So I waited for 45 minutes. When he had not come back I went downstairs and I was hobbling along the road when finally I see him driving down the road. He had left the car lights on so the battery had gone flat. He then ran to a friend's garage a few blocks away to borrow a battery starter. We finally got home so I could have a rest. At the time I was a bit upset but now I laugh about it.

When the IVF did not work we were lucky enough to have been taking care of a friend's twin girls as though they were our own. Bless them. We have also fostered children, although we have decided not to do that anymore.

From my experience with fostering, I believe that caregivers for foster children (even grandparents) should have more rights, as the foster parent is nurturing and loving someone else's child. If the parents are not able to care for their child at that time, then they should get the help they need and prove that it is in the child's best interest to see them.

Although the system is needed—as who knows what would happen to these children if it weren't for this system?— any system can be improved and needs to be updated regularly.

I have also incorporated into my life Birman cat breeding. I love having new kittens in the house, as this fulfills my nurturing role. All the kittens go to very loving homes.

I am here to love, heal, empower others, honor my soul and help heal the world in this lifetime, and children were not part of the plan this time around. I do my best every day to fulfill my part of this agreement.

It doesn't matter what experience you have happening in your life, there is always something positive that comes out of it. It can just take some time to sift through it all. I ask myself, What can I learn from this and how can I do this better next time?

The following chapters are insights and learnings that have come from my own life experiences written from my heart and the reason I am sharing them is to help others and let you know that the world of affirmations, positive thinking and deeper connection truly does work.

For all the blessings that I have received in my lifetime *I give thanks*.

God bless you all.

Our beloved Claude – may he rest in peace

Mooneyes Birmans sealpoint birman kitten called Zebula.

Photo by Helen Westerbeke.

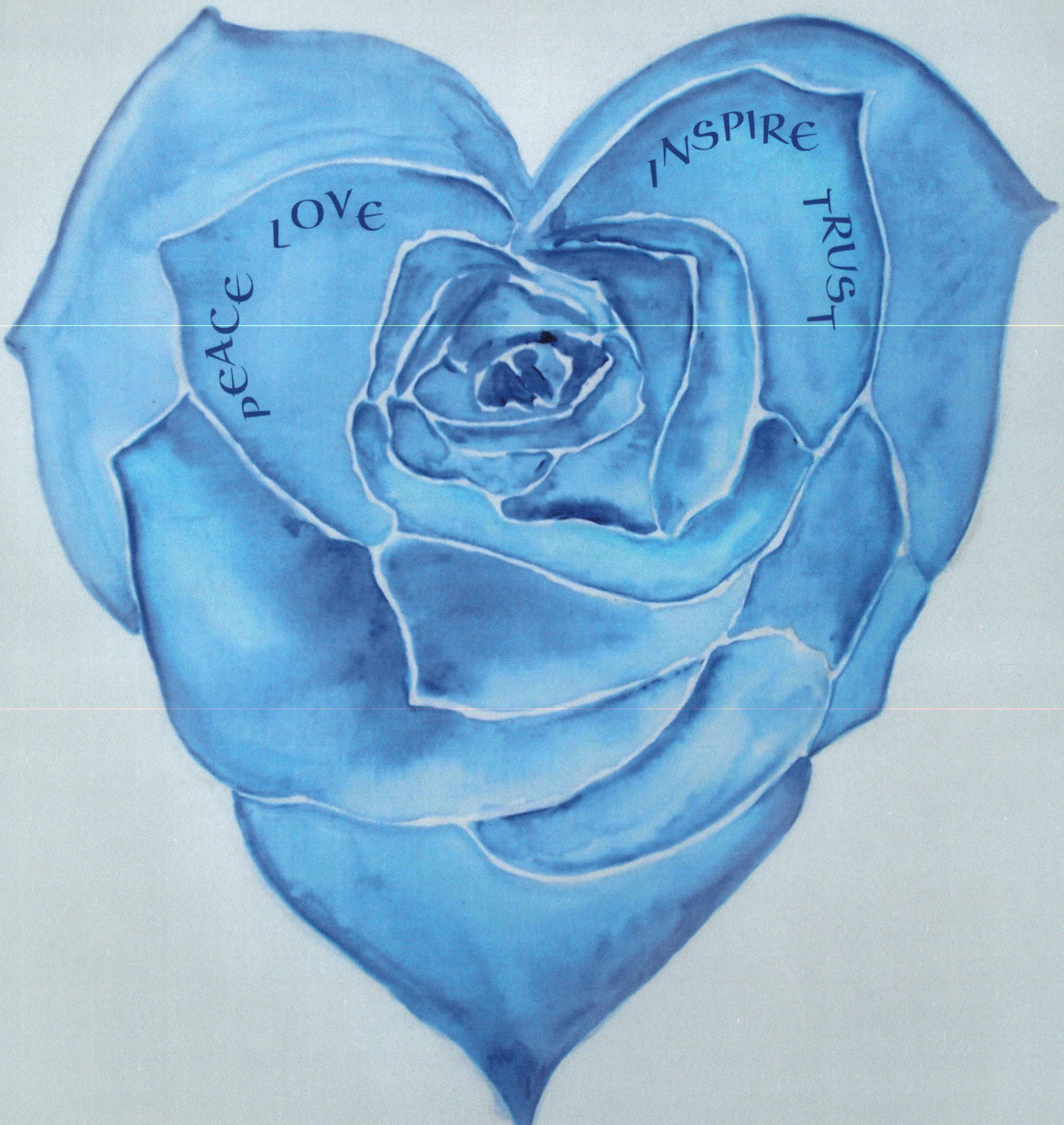
PEACE LOVE
INSPIRE TRUST

Chapter 2: Love

Every human being wants to love and be loved.

Because we have been conditioned in childhood by the adults around us, our limiting belief systems and old programming can hinder us from developing loving relationships and achieving whatever we wish in our lives. Our old thought patterns and behaviors can get in the way of our new life and limit us.

The key to any loving relationship—whether with a partner, friend, mom, dad, brother, sister, family member, boss, employee, colleague, or acquaintance—is first having a deeper understanding and acceptance of yourself. You must have a loving relationship with yourself. You are a very important person in this universe by being you.

If you learn to love and accept yourself unconditionally and understand yourself better, you will grow and things will start happening for you. These must occur, as loving and accepting yourself is like a ripple in a pond, transforming how you think, and the universe has to respond. The book *The Secret* by Rhonda Byrne explains this in more depth.

Love helps us find our way, and when we are loved and supported, it is amazing how high we can soar. If we truly believe we are loved and supported and that we deserve the very best in this world, our vibration changes and in return our life changes.

Love:

> lets go of all fear;
>
> lets go of all doubt;
>
> lets go of all pain;
>
> and helps you move through old limitations and barriers.

There is a song "Love is Letting Go of Fear" on Olivia Newton John's CD *Grace and Gratitude*.

I cannot say enough about love and how important it is in your life. To live without love is not natural and does not fulfill your needs. But this does not mean that you should be in a relationship just to have love. In fact, if you are in a relationship just for the sake of being in one, you might need to do some more work on your relationship with yourself.

If you are in a relationship, open communication is the best way to keep it healthy (especially for women, who like to express their feelings verbally). If both parties are able to communicate with and know what they need from each other, they will get to know and understand each other better and grow together. It takes many years to get to know someone.

The book *Men Are from Mars, Women Are from Venus*, even though it has been around a long time, has very useful, insightful information. I read it to my husband in bed when we are having an issue, and we just laugh because it is so true. (Sometimes, if the issue has not been resolved, I will even read it to him in his sleep.) It is best if you both can accept your differences, embrace your gender, and love who you are and let each other be.

Determine what love means to you, the book "The Five Love Languages" by Gary Chapman can also help with this. Love may mean having your friends and family around, being with your children or whatever it is for you. For me it is spending time with my friends and family, my loved ones. If you would like your partner to have certain qualities then ask yourself if those qualities are within you, for whatever you give out is returned to you. Remember if you work with yourself first then you should notice changes within the people around you. If you need to do more work with yourself, now is the time. Go within and ask for guidance from your source, your devine energy. After a while, an answer will come, but perhaps not immediately. So keep asking until you receive an answer or a sign from the universe. As you visualise your life and how you would like it to go you will notice that you are supported on your path by lots of interconnecting moments, events or people that cross your path to help you on the way. I call these serendipity events. While writing this book I have had many self doubt moments and the universe has always sent me someone or something to restore my faith and keep me on track. The Doreen Virtue "Mary Queen of Angels" came into my life and I pulled the cards "Faith" and "Hope". I had lunch with my mentor Michelle from Inspire Me who said "Believe in Yourself". I also meditate every day and ask for a more extraordinary life and that everything is happening for my highest good and I have faith that everything is working out amazingly for me. You can do the same.

If you would like to have more supportive people around you, affirm that you have people who are kind, loving, and supportive surrounding you, and see where this takes you.

It is important to know there is no right and wrong with love. There is only how you feel and what is right for you in the present. Show your love to the people you care about. If you love someone let them know as you don't know how long you have together. Create loving moments as you spend time together and cherish those moments. Make sure you tell them you love them every day. Forgive them when they upset you and keep sending them love. Love has the power of moving mountains.

If you are a woman who feels it is necessary to give your love away easily, some inner work can help you with your emotional programming and lead you to a more deeper understanding of yourself. If a love relationship is healthy, you will feel no pain, shame, doubt, or fear. Rather, you will be happy and enjoy who you are. If you feel otherwise, it may be time to change something. If you want something to stop you need to let someone know you need help be it a friend or an organisation.

If you decide to release all that no longer serves you, you must continue to daily affirm, "I release all that does not serve me for my highest good." If you are a very responsible person who does not like to let other people down or you take on the responsibilities of the world, this affirmation may not feel comfortable to you. That is good, though, because it is right where you need to be. Keep affirming.

Remember, this is all about *your* life journey. When something doesn't feel comfortable, normally it means you need to work on something inside yourself or you need to let go of something. Just know it will all be okay.

Along with your affirmations, there are homeopathic healers, Reiki healers, holistic healers, massage therapists, and various other types of healers who can help you clear old emotional programming and enable you to sit in your own magnificence, your devine energy. Your inner wisdom coming from a place of love and a willingness to connect deeper with your soul.

Another part of loving yourself is learning to receive. For some people, this is easy; for others, it is not. To be open to receiving, affirm, "Everything comes to me easily and effortlessly" and "I am open to receiving," and see what happens. For me, I started noticing little things. It is amazing what we receive every day that we take for granted.

I am grateful for everything I experience. I am grateful for the little things, the simple things which heightens the beauty in everything for me — a smile, a kind word, the trees, the birds, the grass, the ocean, the sky, everything that nature has to offer—and I express gratitude for everything I have at this time. I know I am meant to be exactly where I am now. Every experience that comes into my life has something to teach me and is for my highest good. For each, I give thanks.

Thank you for making me wiser.

Thank you for teaching me better ways to do things.

Thank you for reminding me how important I am.

Thank you for my good health.

Thank you for providing the food I eat that nourishes my body.

Thank you for my wonderful job and boss who loves and respects me.

Thank you for the opportunities that are given to me.

Thank you for my wonderful healing gifts and my successful healing business.

Thank you for my loving, caring husband.

Thank you for my beautiful home.

Thank you for my beautiful cats.

Thank you for everything that is in my life now.

Thank you for all the joyous experiences that the universe brings into my life every day.

Thank you for my beautiful, kind friends.

Thank you for all the love and support the universe has provided to me when I have needed it.

Thank you for teaching me how to receive.

The more grateful I am, the more abundant my life becomes.

I have spent years working with myself, incorporating the teachings of Louise Hay, as well as working with various other teachers including Sarona Hawkins a Reiki Master in Wellington who worked with me to release old limiting programming and enjoy a deeper understanding of myself through my own personal growth on my spiritual journey. This journey is different for everyone. No one person is the same so never underestimate your journey. This was also when I became a Reiki Practitioner.

I once had a client who had a program she was carrying and perpetuating in her mind that "Everyone thinks I am a bad person. Nobody cares about me." And she would walk around feeling bad about herself and situations would crop up to confirm her thinking. Not only was this not good for her, but it was not true. It was only after she changed the mental pattern and started to affirm to herself "I am a good person", "I love myself" and "Everyone Loves Me" that things started to change. She also had to release a program "I release the need to be punished". I also had similar programing. There are lots of different programs that we all carry but first we need to become aware of them within ourselves before we can do anything about them.

We are all responsible for ourselves in our lifetime. No one else can give us a good life. Only when we stop blaming everyone else and start working on ourselves do we begin to move forward. The first step is loving and being kind to ourselves and working on changing our negative thought patterns to positive ones. For example,

I love myself, therefore … I am surrounded by love.

I am grateful for …

By practising your daily affirmations, you will notice things starting to happen for you no matter how big or small.

Everyday I wake up and I bless my life and say thank you for another day here and I do not want to waste a moment.

I start my gratitude prayers by being grateful for a good night's sleep as I always sleep well.

I am grateful for my husband kissing me goodbye and telling me he loves me as he goes off to work.

I am grateful for my home that I live in and my beautiful kitchen which I cook nutritious healthy meals in.

I am grateful for my job that I work at.

I am grateful for my healing gifts which help people that come to see me.

I am grateful for my loving supportive friends around me.

I ask that my day ahead is smooth and I am able to take things in my stride as they come up.

I am grateful for the deep sense of love and happiness inside me.

I ask that everything happens for my highest good.

I say I love you Tania Thornton, You are a Magnificent Child of the Universe.

I am grateful for all the help and support I am getting to publish this book.

I prosper wherever I turn. Abundance comes to me easily and effortlessly.

I am working with Louise Hay and Cheryl Richardson to help "Heal the World".

These are the affirmations that I use you can also use them or create your own.

Chapter 3: A Mother's Love

Being a mother is much easier if you have a loving, supportive partner, as this relationship can create a solid foundation for the child or children. Raising a family with a supportive partner is a blessing. However, a baby puts much more pressure on a relationship, so you need to be aware of how things are going to work for you and your partner. There needs to be much more open communication, patience and understanding with each other as everyone is learning a new role. There is no manual for being a mother just a whole lot of love and trial and error to find out what works for you and your child.

There are many single mothers, and I say, "Bless you all," as you have undertaken a path that at times will be very difficult and will require far more patience and tolerance both with yourself and your child. But a mother's love for her child somehow manages to overcome most difficulties.

Motherhood is an undervalued role in our society, but it is one of the most important jobs any woman will ever have in her lifetime, as it will dictate how that child turns out. The more support the mother has, the better it is for both her and the child. That child is the future of our world, so it is very important that he or she is given the best start possible.

A mother's unconditional love for her child is something that can never be replaced and is what actually allows the child to grow and become an individual. A mother will sacrifice. I remember my mother would always wait up until I got home to make sure that I was okay. I remember that my mum would lovingly handwash my clothes when I had spilt something on me. My mother would always love me regardless of the silly things that I did or mistakes that I made. I remember when I first met my husband and he would get annoyed about some of the silly things that I did and mum would say "Don't worry Tania, he hasn't had you since you were little". Bless her. Try and remember some of the things that your mother did for you and be grateful for those times that you felt loved. I had no idea of the sacrifices a mother would make for her child until I looked after two beautiful twin girls. That day I became a mother and treated them as my own. Those feelings of wanting to keep them safe and protect them were overwhelming. True unconditional love. We automatically sacrificed – we learnt that it is a great gift to become parents. Please remember that your beliefs as a parent will have a huge influence on your child growing up, so never underestimate your input.

Every child goes through certain stages in his or her life, and at each stage, he or she is able to accomplish certain things. Having patience and great amounts of love, tolerance and understanding is the best possible parenting going through any of the stages with your child. This was really made clear when I did my Certificate of Caring for Children through Stotts Correspondence in New Zealand. This was a two year course and it would benefit any parent trying to get a better understanding of parenthood. Make sure you acknowledge yourself and the wonderful job you are doing. Try not to wait for someone else to tell you how wonderful you are, and just know that you are.

As a mother, remember to reward yourself. This is a very hardworking role, and it is nice to treat yourself with a soak in the bath, a massage, an outing with friends for a break, or whatever it is that recharges your batteries. It is very important that you look after yourself and your needs (when time permits) as well as your child's, as this will improve your relationship with your child.

Affirm: I am always doing the best that I can for myself and my child, and we both deserve the very best in this world.

If for some reason you are struggling with motherhood, as you can become overwhelmed by it, then you may need some help to learn how to take care of your child. Again, making sure that you have a supportive network around you is the key to your learning more and more about being a mother. There are lots of parenting classes and even sharing stories with friends and acquaintances can be enough.

If you do find yourself becoming frustrated as a mother, you need to start asking for help from your partner, friends, or the community support that is available. Remember you need time out as well.

Affirm: I am surrounded and supported by people who love and care about me and my child.

A mother's love should be there for every child. If that wasn't so for you, then there was a reason for this, and it has probably made you a stronger person in some way. You may even have looked up to another adult as a mother figure. There were things that you needed to learn from this experience.

If there are signs that you are carrying blame or resentment from your childhood, then it would be good for you to work on forgiving and on releasing these feelings, as they are very harmful to you.

Affirm: I am able to let go of all my old programs that no longer serve me. I am worthy.

In this day and age, women are far more recognized in the workplace and can easily support themselves. This makes it easier for them to hold down a career and have a family. Women have incredible strength and courage inside them, and when they are able to access this and believe in themselves, they can move mountains and create their dreams. If you believe in yourself and practice personal self-care, life can become easier for you. I have read Cheryl Richardson's book *The Art of Extreme Self-Care*. This is a book that everyone should read.

Affirm: I embrace my femininity and all its power.

Annalise, Vicky and Claude.

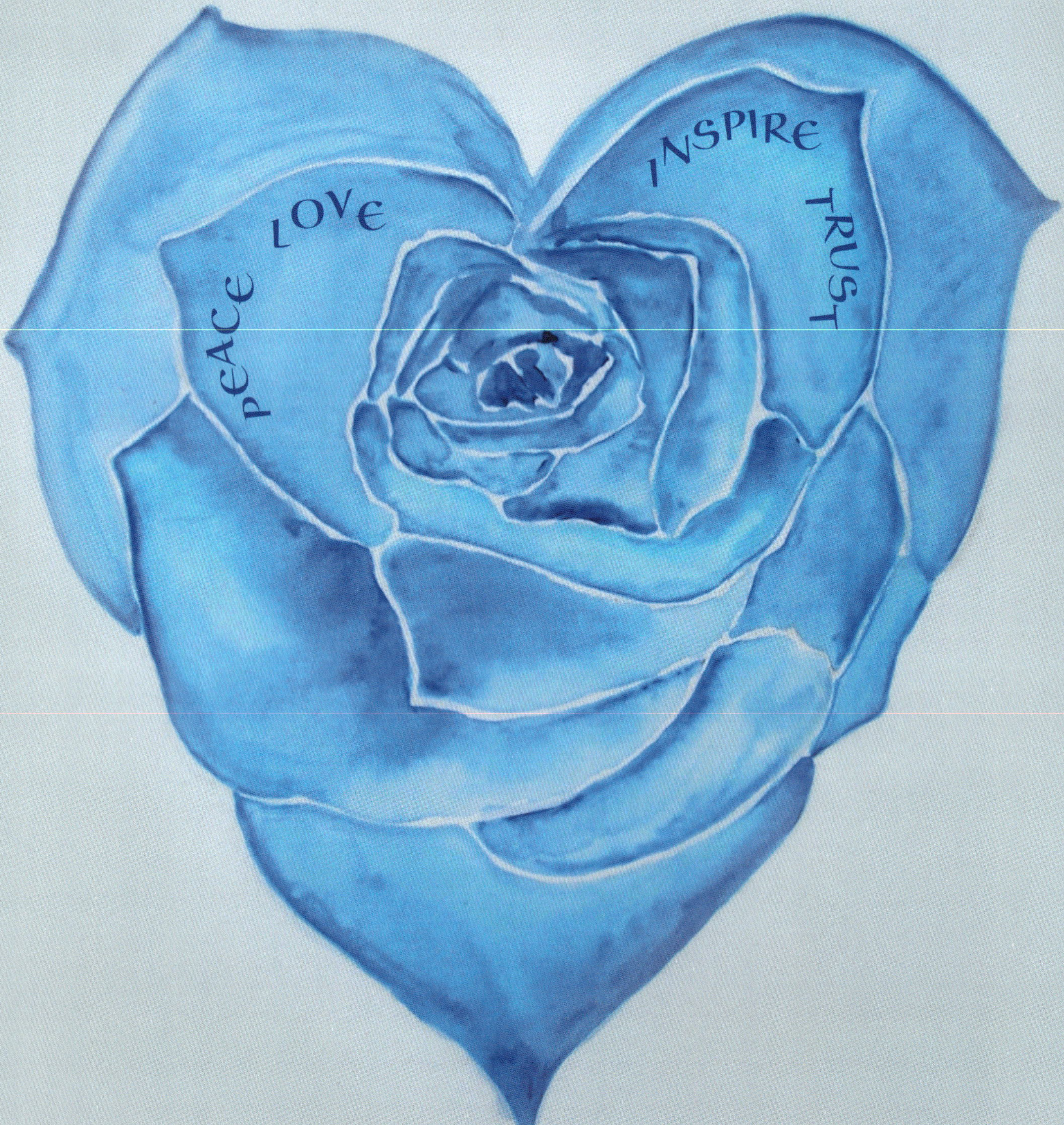
PEACE LOVE
INSPIRE TRUST

Chapter 4: Losing a Child

A parent who loses a child has been dealt one of life's cruelest and most unfair blows. No parent should ever have to bury his or her child, but it does happen.

When we are born our soul has a blueprint already written and although it can be altered during our lifetime, depending on what choices we make, ultimately the universe will keep us on our life path. If it is time for your child's soul to cross, no matter what age he or she is, then know it is their time and they have completed what they needed to do this time around.

While the pain and grief is insurmountable and your heart feels as though it has had the life squeezed out of it and life is very muddled and confusing at this time, there also needs to be an understanding that this was part of that soul's learning and that you were on this earth together for a reason. You have played a big part in that soul's journey, and now it has ended.

There is nothing anyone can do or say, and only time and love can heal. The sense of loss and despair at your child not being protected, and the question "Why my child?" and "Why Me" must be hard to bear.

Just know that your child is protected; that beautiful soul well taken care of once he or she has crossed.

Every soul has a guardian angel who is with them at the time of passing. There is a transition period for the soul to accept the crossing, to be able to move into the light for their next stage of growth and evolving.

Even though I have not had children of my own I have had children in my life who I have loved as though they were my own, true unconditional love, and when those children have left my life I felt a huge sense of loss and felt like my heart would explode and never come right. This also happened when the IVF process did not work, again I had to come to terms with that sense of loss. What worked for me was I learnt to put all that unconditional love into myself. Please know that you are well protected at this vulnerable time as your angels and guides will be there to help you. As I evolved and my life became easier the pain was also easier to deal with. During this time there was a deepening of my connection with spirit. Through this connection with spirit I am able to help people get in touch with their loved ones that have passed over.

If you have lost a child, it is important to allow yourself to grieve, to be kind to yourself, to try not to blame yourself, and to remember your child as you knew him or her and the love that you shared. Make sure that you ask for and receive the help that you need to deal with the loss. Your child will always be a part of you so embrace that part of you and love it. Remember all the gifts that you have received from that child.

You can say to yourself:

I know my child is no longer here with me but I know that he/she is safe and in the light now and his/her memories are always with me.

Chapter 5: Losing Someone Close to You

Losing someone close to you—whether it be your partner, a parent, an immediate family member, or a very close friend—either by death or a relationship break-up this is a traumatic experience, and life will change for you. In your time of grief, you really need to take care of yourself and your body. Make sure you look after and nurture yourself at this time. Be kind to yourself, you have had a relationship with this person and now they are no longer there. Remember, we all deal with things differently, and again there is no right or wrong way when dealing with grief. These things take time and everyone handles grief in a different way. It is important to realise that grief is a natural process of life. We will all cross over one day so just know that this person has started a new part of their journey.

What can help you is remembering the person for who they were, how their life touched you and other people, and what their purpose here was long after their funeral. They were an important part of the universe and their memories should be kept alive. You should also acknowledge your role in supporting them in the time they were here. This is one time in your life when you should ask for help to deal with your loss. We all have guardian angels as well, and if you ask for help they will be there for you.

If something has happened in your life such as a death, a loss, an illness that brings pain and grief, emotions can be brought to the surface that you may not have felt before. It is important not to suppress those emotions and to let them come to the surface. To carry on as though everything is normal can actually do more harm than good. It may feel easier to hide your pain, anger and grief but it really does need to come out before you become a victim of your own grief and your life is just going through the motions. No matter how hard it gets and how bad you feel I know that little by little it does get easier. So never give up. Don't lose your faith. Just know that there is a far greater plan for you.

There does need to be a grieving time, but you can become a victim of your own grief. The emotion of grief can be so overwhelming that it can interfere with your life, your decision making, and your way forward in the world. Even in your time of grief, once over the initial period, you still need to function. At this time people around you may not understand the things you are going through, but they will be there for love and support. Ask for help when needed. Seek counselling if you need to. Join a group-do whatever it takes for you to make sure that you get through this part of your life. Remember you are not alone.

I have personally dealt with a lot of loss in my lifetime both financially and with people I have loved so I know what it is like to become a victim of your own grief. This was not a very healthy way for me to be. With lots of meditation, working with my guides, affirmations, reiki healing, spiritual counseling, massage, vitamins and a good healthy diet and some exercise I have moved forward to a new chapter in my life.

Love knows no bounds, no time, no dimension.

It is inside us.

As we live, we create with love,

kindness, and compassion.

We let you go, knowing that we will

Always hold our love for you in our hearts.

Chapter 6: A Father's Love

A father's love starts off as very proud, beaming. Of course, fathers soon focus on the thought "I must provide for my family." My father worked very hard to provide a home for our family.

A father's support needs to be emotional as well as financial; yes, the whole package is needed for the family unit to function in a healthy way for everyone. A father's role is very important in a family.

Men have their own difficulties and challenges with life and their own inner turmoil, which they may not know how to deal with or express. They can end up more frustrated about things and can easily get grumpy. They are naturally more closed off than women and need their own space.

Becoming a father can be a tough and challenging experience for men, as suddenly they are thrown into a world of chaos and have this little child who is taking their partner's attention away from them. They suddenly have a great deal more responsibility, and they are running around doing their best, learning as they go. Despite all the changes, you can only hope that they are able to communicate with their partners to bring the family unit closer.

Some men are naturals at it, while others take some time to learn, God bless them. And then there are some who seem unable to step up and take responsibility of becoming a parent.

These days there are lots of self-help books and classes that men can attend so that they can get a better understanding of themselves. It would be nice to see more men understand that the little things are important, they don't need to be grumpy and that life is to enjoy

Affirm: I am able to support my family. I am a good dad, willing to learn as I go.

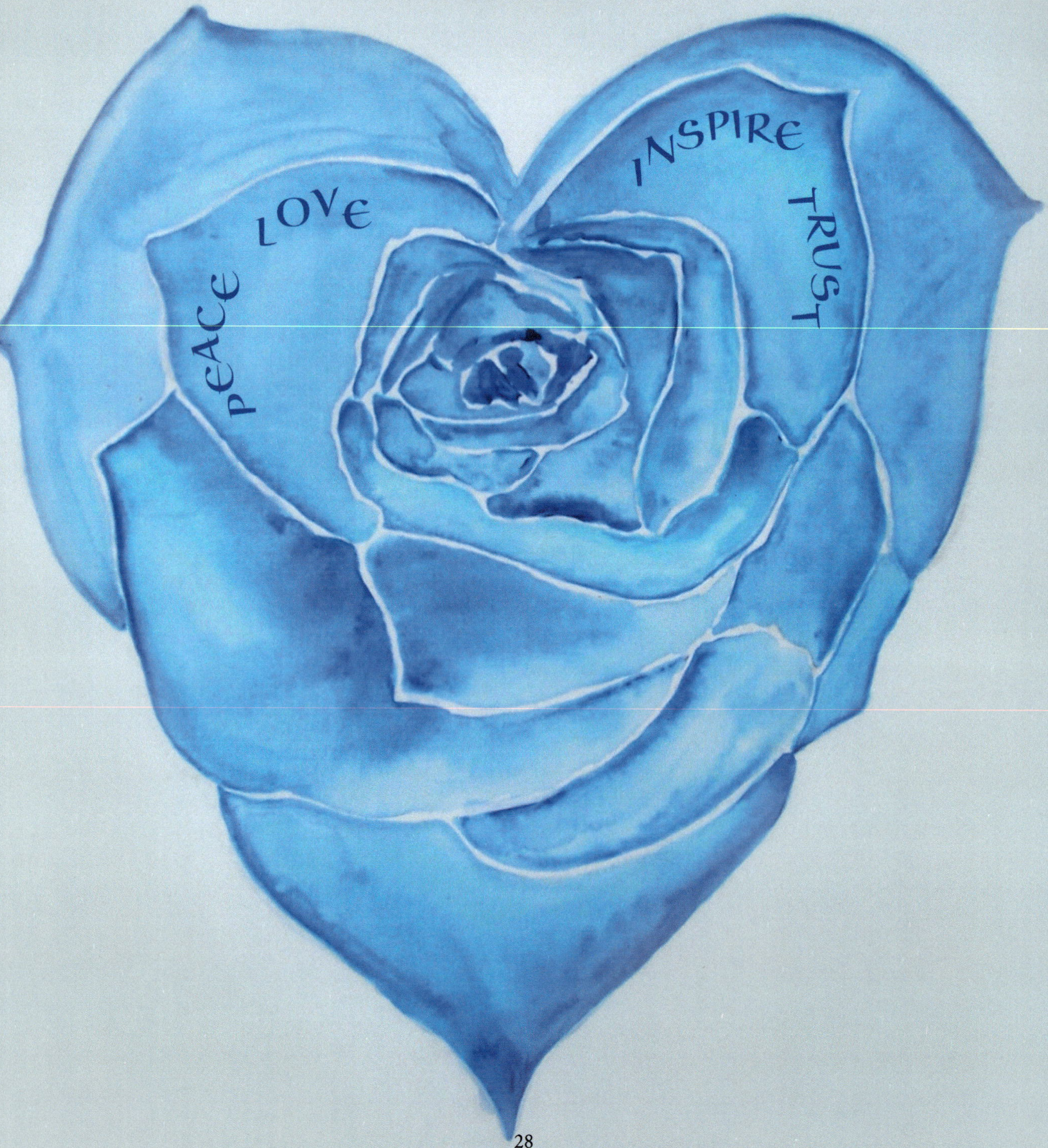
PEACE
LOVE
INSPIRE
TRUST

Chapter 7: A Child's Unconditional Love

A child's unconditional love for his or her parent or grandparent or anyone that he or she can share this love with is indescribable. This emotional bond can make you feel "ten-foot tall and bullet-proof." This love can empower anyone. The trust and the love that they give you is amazing. They accept you just the way you are. I believe that bringing a child into this world is one of the greatest gifts a person could ever receive and that children should be valued and respected from birth.

Remember, the better that you do by them, the better they will do by you. They are the voices of the future, and they learn from the adults around them.

I have never felt as blessed or as loved as I did when I had twin girls to look after. They were the two most beautiful little girls, with lovely little souls and the biggest amount of love. We had the best four years together that anyone could have asked for. We loved them so. I still remember tucking them in at night, reading them stories, playing games with them, helping them with their schoolwork and reading and writing, teaching them how to do craft, giving into them to make them happy, walking along the beach with them, just letting them be themselves and having a lot of fun with them. I guess "True Love cannot be Broken". I give thanks for the time we had with them, for this was special. We all grew in this time together from love. Sadly we have moved in two different directions but I know the love we shared will always be remembered.

We have also been blessed with our goddaughter, Lexi, who is five years old, and my nephew and my niece, Noah (age four) and Ruby (age two). I find children wonderful to be around as they seem to bring out my own inner child; their innocence and the way they come out with things, straight from the mouths of babes, so to speak, is so refreshing. They are themselves in their innocent and carefree way.

As we don't have any children of our own, it is absolutely fantastic to spend time with them and enjoy their company. They have no expectations other than just wanting to spend time with you. Spending time with them is truly one of the most important things a parent can do.

Affirm: I am loved by my family and friends and their children.

Noah and Ruby my nephew and niece

Chapter 8: Your Inner Guidance System

I have had the gift of being clairvoyant since I was very young. I was very sensitive to other people's feelings and moods and I was able to receive messages. As I got older I had an ability to know what people needed. I would also have visions and hear things but did not understand what they were about. It was not until the age of forty that I started to accept this gift as part of my life and developed my intuitive gifts.

As mentioned in my life story, when I was growing up, my gift was not understood in our home as there was a lot of fear around it. It runs in our family. My Aunty had the gift and she was offered to train as a clairvoyant but she had not been allowed. Back then they had thought she was mad so it was not spoken about in our house. It was hard enough trying to express myself as a female. When I became a rebellious teenager, trying to find my way in the world I did not feel that I fitted in anywhere and I did not realise that I had the gift. I really thought there was something wrong with me. It took a long time for me to accept my clairvoyant abilities and through my own experiences and releasing past emotional programming I am able to connect with my guides to help me share my gifts with others to help them heal.

I now do clairvoyant readings for people connecting with spirit to bring their loved ones through or help them with any life issues they may have. I am an open channel for my guides to work through. I am a qualified Reiki practitioner and also a Life Coach using my own life experiences to teach techniques to help clients release and clear past limiting beliefs and programs so they can move forward and deal with the stress of everyday life in a more positive and healthy way.

We are all born with a natural ability to tap into the source of wisdom and psychic knowledge within us. It is this source that the universe responds to. This source knows what is best for you. It is finding a deeper connection to this source that enables miracles to happen. There are lots of books and courses around to help you with this. Listen to your own intuition. Does this feel right or wrong for you right now, should you be here, should you be doing this, and then listen to the answer and act accordingly. Your connection to your own source can depend on how conscious you are and how much attention you pay in each moment. Your thoughts and your words that you speak are the two things that you need to be conscious about as well as the way that you feel. You can start this process by doing meditation or having healings or just taking the time to relax with yourself with some soothing music. Whatever it is that works for you to get that deeper connection with yourself.

Pay attention to your own system.

Connect to your source, your own magnificence and the universe will respond immediately to you.

Meditation is one of the tools that I like to use to start my day to connect with my source. This starts my day off and I ask that my day goes smoothly and all my needs are met easily and effortlessly. I express gratitude for everything I have and I take notice of all the beautiful things around me.

Your intuition is normally spot-on, so listen to it. How many times have you had a gut feeling or a sign and ignored it, and it has turned out to be right?

You are your own best indicator; if it feels right, go with it, and if it doesn't, don't. Listen to alarm bells and then question whether they are true or not. Then make a decision. For safety, I always go with my gut feeling.

Every night before I go to sleep I do a meditation and I ask that myself, my husband and all my loved ones are safe and well and being lovingly protected by the great devine.

I ask that the four archangels stand outside my home at all times protecting me and my family and I know that we are safe and out of harm's way and I am so grateful to the universe for this sense of security. You can do this too it just takes practice.

Chapter 9: Being Present in Each Moment

It is important for every person to be present in each moment yet this does not seem to happen. Our life is made up of a whole lot of treasured moments and opportunities, so it really helps to be fully present for all of them. When you are practicing this, and capturing each moment, you are living your own life to the fullest

Reactions to circumstances can cause you to spiral out of control emotionally, which can lead you to not being present at that time. In this state stress levels can rise and then start a spiral of harmful behavior toward yourself, such as using drugs, alcohol, or food, gambling, spending money, or other destructive behaviors.

If you are a person who can shrug things off easily and have a quick recovery time, good for you, well done.

If you are a person who emotionally reacts, and old patterns and programming resurface, then this may be an opportunity for you to do some inner work and building of your self-esteem and confidence to release old limiting belief systems about yourself. If you need help ask for it. We all get the words "But there are worse people off then you, you are lucky". This may be true but if negative emotions or patterns are coming up for you, you need to deal with them. Otherwise they may cause chaos in your life. If you are in a situation like this yourself, then you can practice the affirmations "I am willing to release old programs that no longer serve me" and "I am thoroughly deserving of the very best in the world."

What I have found is that as you go along, other people can try to reflect their own belief systems onto you or influence you, and you can get caught up in that. Once you stand in your own power and your own integrity and work with your own values, you start to grow as a person and become the person you are meant to be. I often say to myself "It is okay to be me".

We all have an ego, but when the ego becomes the only thing driving you, then, your life is out of balance. When your life is out of balance, decisions you make at that time may not be in your best interests. As we learn to live with love and warmth and build a stronger relationship with ourself our ego starts to breakdown and our higher being takes over.

We all have our own paths to follow and our own ways to learn. We are all responsible for our own happiness in every present moment. What thoughts we choose to think in every moment and what we would like to achieve in our lives are our responsibility.

Once you have decided on the direction that you wish to go, you need to ask to receive, then you need to be present to see the signs of how the universe is working it all out for you. The moments which will propel you to where you wish to go. If they come up and it is easy don't doubt it. If you are waiting, keep asking.

There is a bigger plan; you just may not see it yet. If something is not working for you, then change it; try a different approach or a different action until something falls into place. If something doesn't fall into place, then let it go and leave it, because it may not be the right time for it, or there is something bigger happening behind the scenes. This is when we need to have some patience.

Affirm: I am exactly where I am meant to be; everything is working out perfectly for me.

While I was writing this book I had no idea how it was going to come together, who would publish it, had not even thought about illustrating it and the events that have happened to get it to its final stage just fell into place. The acts of grace just happened.

Chapter 10: Stress

We live in a world where everyone is so busy competing with each other, and so busy trying to get ahead, that stress is everywhere. We do not need to fight and compete for things, and if we all worked together as one, then everything would become much easier.

I personally believe that there is enough in this world for everyone. I am always taken care of financially, and I am always supported by the universe.

If you are living with stress, then it is important that you find out what works for you to relax and how you can manage your stress. Some stress is healthy, because you do need to know that you are alive.

When stress is overwhelming you, it is time to do something about it. I like to take nice walks in the park, visit the duck pond, meditate, have a massage, have a bath, and spend some time with my husband watching the planes come in and go out at the airport down at Lyall Bay in Wellington.

I find that meditation and my daily spiritual practices help. Staying in the moment and using my affirmations "I am okay," "Things are okay for me," and "I am safe" work for me.

Exercise is something that helps relieve stress and is good for keeping your body healthy. It makes you feel good afterward. I have never been one to feel good *during* exercise, but I still make an effort to go to the gym. You need to find a form of exercise that works for you.

Stress can cause long-term damage to your body, so to minimize it you need to find out what works to de-stress you. Vitamin B can also help with stress.

I find your breath can calm you down as well. When things become a little overwhelming, I catch myself and start to take deep breaths. This brings me back into the present moment.

It is also important not to get caught up in someone else's stress or drama, as there are people who are always trying to hook you in. Take care of yourself first. Follow your own instincts and do not go there if it is not for you. If the situation is real then compassion and understanding takes over and you may wish to offer to help.

Affirm: I can deal with any situation easily. I am capable of taking things in my stride. I am my own person.

Chapter 11: Your Mind and Your Body's Ability to Heal Itself

The human body has the knowledge and capability to heal itself. Unfortunately, though, through stress, outside influences, and addictions, your body sometimes is unable to do its job by itself and needs some help. You can create your own illnesses, and I refer you again to Louise Hay's *How to Heal Your Life*. Carrying emotional wounds or old limiting beliefs that no longer serve you can create illness in your body. Of course, you should always seek medical advice from your doctor if you think there is something wrong. There is a place for the medical profession as well as holistic medicine.

Healthy thoughts lead to a healthy body. Healthy food and nutrition makes a healthy body that can then take care of itself. These days there are so many processed, unnatural foods on the shelves of the supermarket that create toxins in our bodies, which can lead to cancer and all sorts of serious illnesses. If you have been diagnosed with a serious illness, your type of treatment will be up to you. Looking within and coming to terms with and clearing your past can help heal you.

We all need to eat more natural and raw foods, anything that you can recognize as real food. We also need to be more aware of what we are putting into our mouths and be more vigilant about reading food labels. We also need to think about what we are putting into our children's mouths. Sugar can play havoc with your body as well as your mood.

Our thought processes play a big part in our health and can help to manifest illness. Letting go of feelings of resentment, bitterness, pain, and blame can heal your body. Emotional well-being plays a big part in the way our bodies feel. Listen to your body if you are feeling stressed or your body is feeling unwell: listen to it. There is a reason for this. Be kind to yourself and listen for the insights that will come to you from listening to your body. Inna Segal has a book called *The Secret Language of Your Body* that tells you more about this subject.

I think it is amazing that our cells can rejuvenate themselves, our liver can regenerate, and we have a natural immune system that fights off infection. Your body is made to look after itself; you just have to let it.

I have battled with my weight my entire life, which had a lot to do with the way I was living and the amount of stress that was in my life. After recently losing 25 kg over a period of around 6 months I am finally at a weight that I love and I feel healthy. I am also embracing my femininity and enjoying this part of my life and hope you can too.

I am really enjoying my new way of eating and learning all about how food affects me. Growing your own vegetables or eating organic is the way to go if you are able to do so. We need to take the time and put the effort into obtaining the knowledge to look after ourselves. You can find so much knowledge on the internet these days. You only need to search about organic foods, or establishing your own garden, or learning about places to go to exercise, and so much information comes up. There are so many ideas and products it is just a matter of finding out what works for you.

We need to love ourselves enough to want to take care of ourselves and our loved ones the best we possibly can.

Chapter 12: My Healing Gifts

My life has given me a lot of insight and wisdom from a very young age. I have also been given the ability to help heal people which has been developed over my lifetime. I know that leading by example and having a more conscious life, I am able to fulfill my soul purpose here and I hope that you are able to do the same.

I have experiences in my life where no day is the same. My husband says that every day is a surprise. I love going with the flow and spontaneity; this happens a lot in my life. I find myself on my own adventures every day and will cross paths with someone who has just lost a loved one, or is in need of a helping hand, or just needs to hear a kind word. I have people come to my home for readings to connect with their loved ones, healings, spiritual counseling and life coaching to clear limiting beliefs.

I have had many experiences where spirit have let me know they are here with me. I have had jugs start boiling for no reason. I have seen picture frames fall down and have put them back up only to have them fall down again. I have spirits visit me in my home and lots of messages come through.

A nun once came to see me. Her sister had passed away, and she had not seen her before she passed. This brought up feelings of guilt for her. It is important to know that the dead don't get caught up in guilt. They have passed on and are in a new dimension and a different space. It also came out that this woman was being bullied at her nunnery by some of the other nuns. Through my guides I did some healing with her, she left feeling much better and a bit stronger.

I have had a client come to me with the lost souls of two children attached to her, and through my guides I have detached the souls and asked them to cross over. The client said that she felt happier, lighter and more at peace.

Another client had AIDS, and I was able to give her a reading and healing. We are still in the early stages of learning about AIDS, but I do believe that loving yourself is a big part of getting better.

I have done many readings while I was in Brisbane and have sat in many circles through the Spiritualist Church in Sydney. I have also been able to do healings on people to help them release their limiting beliefs and attachments to things that no longer serve them working with my guides and using reiki healing.

While I was working with my Reiki teacher, I found out that her mother was very ill with cancer. Not long after that she passed away. Messages from her mother came through for her and helped her be more at peace with her mother's crossing.

I remember doing readings at the Spiritualist Fair and I had a lady walk up to me and I could feel her before she got to me, this overwhelming feeling of grief. She had just lost her sister and had not had a chance to say goodbye and wanted to connect which did happen.

Be grateful for the time that you had left with your loved ones, and just know that when their time comes, they are safe and off onto a new part of life.

Through being an open channel many messages have come through from people's loved ones to help them in their time of grief. Over the years I have been able to do readings and healings for lots of lovely, beautiful souls. I have so many stories of so many people that have come to see me that unfortunately I am unable to write about all of them. I am very grateful to be blessed to be able to work in the field of healing and helping people.

Insights from the Heart was created in my healing room at home.

Just recently I was sent a letter from Qantas advising me that I had to use my airpoints by a certain date or I would lose them. A couple of days later I received an email from Michelle at the Inspire Me store in Palmerston North saying that Hay House was having an "I Can Do It" seminar in Melbourne and Louise Hay would be speaking. The accommodation was booked and that first in could stay with them.

Something woke me up, tapped me on the shoulder and said you need to pay attention to this. I knew right then and there that I was going. I quickly emailed back saying that I would love to take one of the two spaces left, and then I booked my flights and my ticket to the conference. Wow! I couldn't believe that I was on my way to a Louise Hay conference with three strangers. It all felt so spontaneous and unplanned. It felt fantastic. I was so excited! I don't know how it happened but suddenly I had all this energy which helped me to get this book together.

We had been told that when we touched down in Melbourne, we should look out for Michelle and Marea and the angel wings on their backs. Sure enough, we found them because we caught sight of the angel wings. What a hoot. We had all found one another and were off on our new adventure.

Having never stayed in a backpackers before, it was very refreshing to stay at Urban Central Apartments and mingle with the young people. Of course it was not without mishap, as when we got there we had one set of bunks in the room and two single beds. That was okay. In fact, it was much better than we had envisioned. There was one power point and a kettle with a very short lead. So using our Kiwi ingenuity, we put someone's suitcase under the kettle whenever the jug needed to be boiled, so that the cord could reach.

It is very cold in Melbourne at that time of the year, and the room was freezing. The window was stuck open, and it took quite a lot of strength to wind it shut (we were hoping the knob wouldn't break off). The air-conditioning unit did not seem to be working, and the more we tried to fix it, the more cold air seemed to blow out. It was time for action, so we rang downstairs and they said that someone would be up shortly. As we were staying in a backpackers, we were not so sure about this. But within ten minutes, up came this lovely, friendly handyman to help us.

He fiddled with the air-conditioning unit for some time, and it didn't seem fixable. After about half an hour he came back with a heater, an extension cord, and four blankets. We were so grateful for this, and we blessed him. After that he was like our own personal handyman for the weekend. It was all perfect.

The shower was another thing. It had a timer on it, and we could not get it to work. After numerous attempts to get it going, we found out that we had to push a button to get it started and pull the tap out. Twelve minutes per shower was the allowance. You know, it is amazing what you can do in twelve minutes! I was showered and dried, and had my face on and my hair drying, before my twelve minutes were up.

We had four ladies who had come together for this amazing weekend, and there was not one time where we felt like we got in the way of each other.

The I Can Do It seminar was amazing. I bought so many books that I had to pay excess luggage on the way back. I waited in a long line to get Louise Hay's signature and to finally meet the lovely lady who has been my inspiration for so many years. We spent two days listening to some of the most empowering speakers in the world, and I came back feeling fulfilled and fantastic. Thank you, Melbourne. Thank you to my roommates Julie, Michelle, and Marea. Thank you to Louise Hay, Cheryl Richardson, Robert Holden, Suze Orman, Doreen Virtue, Don Miguel Ruiz, and Neal Donald Walsch. I am so grateful for the experience. Bless you.

I am on my spiritual journey and love sharing my insights and inspirations with you which is why this book was created. It starts with looking within. I have found that using daily affirmations, giving and receiving a whole lot of love, and working with my guides and angels has made some wonderful improvements in my life. Thank you for this.

Inspiration:

Trust that life brings you whatever you need in every moment.

Be grateful for everything you have, no matter how big or how small.

Love yourself, whatever situation you may be in at the present time.

Louise Hay and Cheryl Richardson's book *You Can Create an Exceptional Life* is a must-read.

Cheryl Richardson's book *The Art of Extreme Self-Care* is also a must-read, and Cheryl Richardson was a great speaker.

Cheryl Richardson says in her book: Extreme Self-Care Challenge: Falling in Love with You.

Doreen Virtue was a "wow" speaker. Her book *Daily Guidance from Your Angels* is a beautiful must-read.

The seminar was very powerful, and I took a lot from it. You can do it. Just set your mind to it. Visualize it and see what happens.

I say: When you can say "I love myself and want to take care of myself because I am worthy and know that feeling of love and magnificence inside me," then your journey is beginning and you can stand in your magnificence, your true power and reflect this to others.

Chapter 13: Your Spiritual Journey

We are all here on a spiritual journey. As we grow and take up certain roles in the physical, then illusions are created about people's class and worth. In reality our souls are on their own journey, learning and evolving as they are in the physical world.

We are all part of the universe as one, connected and intertwined, and if we could only use that power to help one another rather than hurt and take advantage, life would be a lot happier and easier. Why does it take a natural disaster like an earthquake to make people sit up and take notice and help out? We are all here to help one another. If you need help, you should ask for it. A lot of our world is made up of power games between people, which can create a lot of resentment and unhappiness. On a bigger level, this can even create wars.

Respecting yourself and loving yourself are the two best recipes for standing in your own power.

Every soul has a lifetime of learning and every soul has its own unique way of perceiving, acting, and interpreting what is going on for them.

You have your guides and guardian angels around you as you move through your life journey. These guides are there to help you. You need to ask for their help. Your guides are always trying to communicate with you. In fact, they like singing and having fun. They also like being around you when you are more relaxed and not stressed; otherwise, they find it more difficult to communicate with you. In return, that makes it harder for you to tap into your intuition, or sixth sense.

If you are starting out on this journey, just practice with it, and see what works for you. Everyone has angels that are on hand, just waiting to be asked for help. No one is truly alone.

Whatever your role is here in the physical, we are all still human beings, and we have emotions that we deal with every day. Raw emotion is something that should be embraced as part of you and dealt with as part of your healing process. If overwhelming emotions are triggered, then you may need some help to release them. Reiki, holistic healing, meditation, yoga, and getting in the bath may benefit you. It is only when we try to suppress these emotions and not acknowledge our wounds that we can manifest illnesses in our body or act out because something has not been expressed.

We can also create situations by how we are thinking, so it is best to think many positive thoughts during the day about everything. The one thing you do have control of is the way that you think. Blaming other people is only giving your power away.

As we grow and change and transform, we need to embrace the changes that are happening in our lives and be grateful every step of the way until we settle into our new way of thinking and being. We are all souls on a human journey, evolving and changing as we walk along. If you are happy with yourself, then just acknowledge that and be truly grateful for everything you have.

It takes a whole lifetime to learn, grow, learn some more, and grow some more, using our own pain and suffering to evolve. The pain we have felt in our lifetime helps us to understand more about ourselves and gives us a lot more understanding, empathy, patience, and compassion for others.

Stop comparing yourself to anyone else. You are on your own journey, and it is important to love yourself as you are right now.

Releasing your judgment of others and allowing them to be who they are, is your acceptance of allowing yourself to be free. If someone has done something openly to hurt you, then let him or her go. When the time is right, bless that person and say thank you, for that person will have been a gift sent to help heal you.

Agreements have been made with others before they even come into your life. You draw to you what you need to learn, painful or loving experiences. Remember everyone is playing their role to the best of their ability so that we can all evolve within ourselves.

Always love yourself and be kind to yourself, no matter what life brings you. I do believe that you are given only what you are able to handle at any one time so breathe and let the process happen. We are stronger than what we think.

Chapter 14: Dreams Can Come True

Our conditioning in childhood can inhibit us from following our dreams. The doubts creep in, the lack of confidence or self-belief. Or the "I don't deserve this" or "Someone else deserves this more than me", "I am not good enough" or "I haven't suffered enough yet". These are old limiting belief systems that have been conditioned into you from the time you were very young. I had a teacher at school and when I was about 13 I can remember she told me "That I would never amount to anything". I laugh at that one now.

You actually do deserve the very best in the world. You were born to deserve the very best in the world. Stop doubting yourself: if you believe it is right for you, then yes, it is right for you. Do not question it any more, take your own power back, and follow your inner guidance system.

When you focus on what you want and start talking about it, then you can make it happen. Notice the things you want rather than what you don't want.

When you start to believe in yourself and empower yourself, you will notice that people around you start to treat you differently or that something good happens. If there are people around you who are not there to help and support you evolve then eventually they will fall out of your life.

That is just how it has to happen. Loving, respecting, and believing in yourself are the most important qualities in transforming you. With life's ups and downs there are always opportunities to follow your dreams. However big or small that dream may be.

The way to start the transition to your new way of being is to start writing things down, start to notice the beauty around you, be grateful for the simple things, and take the actions needed to manifest your dreams. Ask for your dream to happen, be clear about what it is and take action when synchronicity moments present themselves to you. Have patience as everything happens in perfect devine timing.

When I was eighteen I hated the thought of traveling anywhere, and if anyone had told me that I would change countries twice, own my own home, get married at the Venetian Hotel in Las Vegas on the Gondola, go to Disneyland and San Diego for my honeymoon, have a very supportive and loving husband, a good job while also running a successful healing business, be successful at breeding birmans and be publishing my first book, I would never have believed it.

If we can think it

We can create it;

If we can dream it

We can be it.

Everyone can create their own dreams.

Our Wedding Venetian Hotel Las Vegas

Lexi driving the Fire Engine in her words she wants to be a "Fire Girl."

Chapter 15: Money

I firmly believe that I always have enough money. I have had that belief since my youth. As already said in My Life Story, when I was around twenty, I won ten thousand dollars on a radio program and on the flip side when my marriage split up I was left repaying my husband's debt. I know what it is like to be on both sides of the coin. I have learnt that money is a means of exchange, and I know that I always have an unlimited amount of money to meet my needs, as the universe is plentiful and I am very deserving of receiving money as is everyone. What you believe about money can influence your whole life. Again in Louise Hay's book "How to Heal Your Life" there is a whole chapter on money. My husband won $2,000.00 on Lotto after reading the book "Money and the Law of Attraction" by Esther and Jerry Hicks just by breathing in money.

Having won and lost money and other events that have happened in my life I have learnt that it is how we treat people that is most important and what we give out always comes back to us. Below are some events that happened in my life to confirm this.

I remember once in Sydney I left my wallet on a seat at the Parramatta train station and it had around $345.00 in it. I got to work and realized I didn't have it. I rang the train station and do you know that it had been handed in and I got all my money back. This has happened to me a couple of times in my lifetime. Another time I was travelling on the train and I found someone's mobile phone and after ringing a name in the phone I tracked down the owner and was able to return the phone to her. She gave me $50.00 because I had done that for her.

There was another time when I had to take a taxi from Sydney CBD to Bondi Junction and I got in a taxi and some man asked if he could get a lift as well so I said yes. When the taxi stopped he got out and rather rudely offered me $1.00 to help pay for the fare. I looked at him and I sincerely said "Don't worry I've got this one" and with that his attitude changed, he looked at me and he said "One day when I have some money I will return the favour and help someone else". And this is what it is all about, when you can help someone please do, that is how the universe, the higher dimension works. I am sure that everyone has stories similar to this. Embrace them and be very grateful for them.

I have affirmations all over my house: "I am worthy of the very best in the world," "My income is constantly increasing," "Money comes to me easily and effortlessly," "I am the luckiest person in the world," "Abundance happens to me everywhere I turn." "I am wealthy".

I love money and money loves me; we have a reciprocal relationship, a means of exchange. You can also exchange services, it does not always have to be money, so long as the parties are in agreement.

Most of my life I spent as an independent young woman supporting myself and surviving. I was always able to get good jobs and work hard for the things that I needed, which for me in itself was a sense of achievement. I still had my own life issues and challenges, and sometimes life could be quite lonely. But I always knew that I would have plenty of money to meet mine, my husband's and my loved ones' needs plus more, and I always have. I spent a long time by myself after my first marriage getting to know myself and I am now very grateful to be with my husband. We recently had a holiday to Fiji, and we took food to one of the orphanages there. They were so grateful to receive the food that it was a blessing for us. It's nice to know that we are able to give to children where we can.

I am now in a loving relationship, and we are able to give to each other and ourselves lovingly now, as money is plentiful and we can enjoy the fruits of our labour.

Money does not make you happy—only you can do that for yourself—but it certainly enables you to make more choices in life and makes things easier. We are all able to change our beliefs about money if we choose to.

Chapter 16: Relationships

The more loving relationships you have in your life, the better life is for you. If you have a partner and a life together, then cherish that. Cherish the heart that loves you. Kindness and compassion are the keys to unlocking the door inside you. You can never hear the words "I Love You" too many times. I know that I never tire of saying or hearing those words.

Relationships are to be worked on every day and the more you give of yourself in a relationship the deeper it becomes. Misunderstandings happen and little things can become big things without too much effort. It is best to try to keep misunderstandings at a minimum and communicate openly without fear. When we are able to work with ourselves, look into ourselves, and start to love ourselves, then the relationships around us have to change or they will diminish.

The more time you spend together, the more you learn about each other, your partner's habits or behaviors, and how to work together. It can take time to accomplish this, and each party must be willing to participate. You and your partner can do exercises together to develop and strengthen your relationship. Listening is the key to better relationships.

When Wayne and I first got together we spent the first two years in the honeymoon stage trying to please each other and pretending we were perfect. After this period there was a time when things started to become a struggle for us as we were working each other out. At times I did ask myself why I was still there, he probably did to. But when you love someone you stick it out and you believe that it is going to get better. We have both evolved in our relationship through love and trust and have started to put ourselves first. Once this happened the arguments started to become less and things became easier. I have also become a lot calmer about things which somehow has helped Wayne. Remember work on yourself first if you want anything to change.

I have learnt that one of the things that makes a happy marriage is a List. In his words "He has no idea what to do for me that will make me happy but if I write a list he knows." If you expect him to know, he doesn't. If you expect him to say something that you want to hear he probably won't. I say to him that when he comes home he needs to leave his work at work and when he walks through the door he is to talk to me and listen to me because he loves me. I also have a lot more patience now and it has taken some years but we are flowing very well together. Remember praise and encouragement works better than anger and screaming. We both say that we have become nicer people to be around.

My husband and I make the effort to keep it interesting, we have both been married before and through those experiences are a lot wiser about how we treat each other. We make time and put effort into our relationship, we spend time together and try to talk things through with each other as best we can. We never go to sleep on an argument and my husband always says "the highlight of his day is cuddling up together at night".

When you are in a loving, supportive relationship, you feel empowered, your confidence grows, and you are able to soar like an eagle. Then you know that no matter what life throws at you, your relationship is strong, and you will work things out together. This should not be taken for granted. A strong relationship must be worked on every day in order to thrive. Remember, tend to your own garden first, and it will grow.

Make sure that when you say you are going to do something you get it done. Make sure that you are able to speak but also to listen. Be careful of the words that you speak. Make sure that you spend quality time together and enjoy just being with each other. Remember you don't know how long you have got together. Make sure you show your love for each other. Never take each other for granted and always do your best no matter what. In any relationship the foundation needs to be strong. As we have not been able to have our own children we now have a saying to each other:

During our time together we are here to help make each other's lives happier and endeavour to live our dreams through love, support, kindness, understanding, patience and forgiveness keeping our relationship open and loving. It is amazing how True Love makes you feel secure. Making Love is a Gift of this Love.

The biggest thing a man can ever do is listen to his woman.

A woman needs to make sure her man really knows that his work is appreciated and that he is loved.

There is a Cherokee Proverb:

A Man's Highest Calling is to Protect Woman so she is free to walk the earth unharmed.

A Woman's Highest Calling is to lead a man to his soul to connect him with source.

Affirm: I have more loving relationships with my partner, family and friends. My family, friends and everyone love me.

Loving Words from My Husband

My darling Tania.

I take you to be my partner in life and my one true love.

I will cherish our union and love you more each day.

I will trust you and respect you, laugh with you and cry with you, loving you faithfully through good times and bad, regardless of obstacles we may face together.

I give you my hand and my heart from this day forward for as long as we both shall live

Loving Words from my Wife

My darling Wayne

I love you with all my heart and only wish the best for you.

I will do my best every day to help you and look after you as you are the most thoughtful and kind man that I have ever known.

I treasure each moment that we have together as long as we both shall live.

PEACE LOVE INSPIRE TRUST

Chapter 17: Friends

I believe that in your lifetime friends will come and go. I have learned a lot from my friends over the years, and I have had and still have many friends. A wise lady once told me that if you can get to the end of your life and you can count 5 people who are still your true friends then you are lucky.

I believe that there are people that are always there for you, no matter what, helping you and you helping them. Then there are the people that are there only if you are doing something for them. There are also ones that are there to teach you lessons and to help you evolve as a person. When lies and deceit become part of a friendship it is time to move on. You can release them with love. It's the same with any situation that you find yourself in, whether it be with friends or family: bless the situation with love, release it, and let it go to the angels.

I now ask for friends that have the same kind of integrity that I do, that have the same sense of nurturing that I do, and whose intentions are for my highest good. I ask that I am surrounded by friends who love me and whom I love, friends who have my best interests at heart and I have theirs. I also ask for friends that I can laugh and have fun with.

I am loved by everyone. The world loves me.

PEACE LOVE INSPIRE TRUST

Chapter 18: Wounds

My brother had a car accident about 8 years ago where he was left both physically and emotionally injured. He became very ill and my eyes and ears have been opened, and I wrote this poem on wings of love for my brother when he was in hospital, very sick in the ICU.

Your wounds are there for all to see

As you fight for your life,

Your soul deciding to live or die.

Your angels comfort you while you lie there sleeping.

We have lived through your wounds every day.

They represent our past.

And we now understand that you were sent to help us.

And now we ask that your angels protect you in your time of need and help you to restore the light and love inside you.

We cannot fix your wounds of old.

But we can start again as each new moment unfolds.

We create in love

And can only do our best

And ask that healing is happening in your time of rest.

God bless.

My brother survived and although he is still very ill when he woke up he said:

"You know Tania before this happened I really didn't care if I lived or died, but now I know that I do care and I want to live".

If this was your last day here how would you like to be living it.

Author

Tania Thornton

Email: tania@insightsfromtheheart.co.nz

PO Box 9968, Marion SQ, Wellington, New Zealand

Website: www.insightsfromtheheart.co.nz

Book Illustrated by Artist Maureen McWilliams

Recommendations to help you Evolve:

Kira Kay - www.kirakay.com.

Suzanne Skyring – metaphysically@bigpond.com

Recommendation for Website Design - www.dezignscene.co.nz
The Web Designer that listens, cares about what You want, creates a website that truly represents You and Your business and transforms your online marketing Dreams into Reality.
"Your Success is My Success..." lynda lee

Notes

Notes

CPSIA information can be obtained
at www.ICGtesting.com
Printed in the USA
LVIW021952080413
328178LV00001B